BE FREE. BE YOU.
21 LETTERS TO A BEAUTIFUL AND GODLY LADY

ROXANNE DIXON, ED.D

Edited by KATHARINE WHITELOCK
Photography by KATLYNE HILL
Foreword by BISHOP GLENN B. ALLEN, SR.

DR. ROXANNE DIXON

CONTENTS

Acknowledgments	v
Foreword	vii
Introduction	ix
1. Anger	1
2. Anxiety	6
3. Apologizing	11
4. Baggage	16
5. Comparison	22
6. Courage	27
7. Delays	32
8. Disappointment	37
9. Doubt	43
10. Enemies	48
11. Failure	53
12. Faith	58
13. Fear	64
14. Kindness	69
15. Obedience	76
16. Obstacles	82
17. Perserverance	87
18. Quitting	93
19. Trust	99
20. Weight	104
21. Thank You	110
22. Prayer	115
23. Notes	116

All rights reserved. No part of the publication may be reproduced, stored in a retrieval system or transmitted in any form, or by any means, electronic, mechanical photocopying, recording or otherwise, without written permission from the publisher.

Unless otherwise noted, all Scripture is taken from the King James Version of the Bible.

Copies of this book are available at quantity discounts for bulk purchases.

For more information, contact:

Dr. Roxanne Dixon

www.drrox.org

E-BOOK ISBN: 978-1-7361443-0-5
PRINT ISBN: 978-1-7361443-1-2
Manufactured in the United States of America

ACKNOWLEDGMENTS

I first want to acknowledge God, my Heavenly Father, that anointed me with a ministry of encouragement. It is because of His love, His strength, and His power that I am able to share testimonies and be transparent before you. I am grateful to be used and do not take it for granted. I am forever His child.

Thank you to my mother, Mattie Wells, for not just sacrificing that I may have; but for being a role model of what I can become. You are my number one cheerleader and I love and appreciate you with all my heart.

To my Pookie, Nia Burke, who has been my *purpose* since the day she was born. You have changed my life for the better and I am honored to be your mother.

To all of my siblings, Constance, Curtis, and Randy: Who could have asked for better siblings? Each of you have mentored and molded me in a special way. It is because of the road you paved before me that I am able to enjoy this journey.

To my Bishop, Glenn B. Allen, Sr., who provided a living example of what faith looks like. I will never forget your advice telling me to "jump" when I was afraid to leap. I have been jumping ever since.

To my sister friends, my vault friends, and my crew: Thank you for your support in this process. It has been a long time coming and you never allowed me to quit. You kept the vision before me and I am forever grateful.

———

Last but not least, I want to give special acknowledgment to my husband, Minister Anthony Dixon. Thank you for loving me, supporting me, and coaching me to keep going. I appreciate who you are and all that you are. God created you just for me.

FOREWORD

Dr. Roxanne Dixon is an anointed woman of God and I have had the pleasure of watching her grow both spiritually and professionally. She has a heart for encouraging and empowering women of all ages, and is anointed to do so. This book, *BE FREE. BE YOU: 21 LETTERS TO A BEAUTIFUL AND GODLY LADY* is masterful in its delivery for showing the "B. A. G. Lady" (Beautiful and Godly Lady) that she is not in the struggle of life alone. Roxanne is extremely transparent in sharing with women her own life's struggles and how she navigated through it. As her Bishop, I am extremely proud to see how she is submitting to God's perfect will for her life and allowing her test to be a testimony to others.

In this dispensation of time, this is a powerful message for our young ladies trying to find their way and purpose and for the mature ladies who are wondering if they're on the right track. Dr. Roxanne ends each letter by saying "Onward!" meaning keep pressing forward. She is persistent in reminding us that the vicissitudes of life will occur; but God will never leave us nor forsake us and He has equipped us with every tool we need to keep going.

Her words of encouragement are Holy Spirit inspired and anointed by God. I'm so very proud to say that Dr. Roxanne Dixon is

FOREWORD

my spiritual daughter and co-laborer. Follow this mighty woman of God on this journey to empowerment. I am more than confident that God has so much more to pour out of her.

Fully Persuaded,
Bishop Glenn B. Allen, Sr.,
Founding Pastor
Destiny Christian Center International, Fayetteville, GA

INTRODUCTION

Father, I thank you for the opportunity to share and be transparent with your Beautiful and Godly Ladies. I pray that each page is anointed for your purpose and you get the glory through it all. Bless each woman that reads from the beginning of the book to the end of the book. I declare and decree healing, restoration, and reconnection to take place. Father, I ask that you tear down, root up, and destroy any demonic forces, generational curses, or spiritual strongholds that are holding your daughters back from living the life of purpose and destiny that you have created and ordained them to have. Release gifts, talents, and your anointing to flow like rivers of living water. We give you all the praise and glory in it all, through it all, and for it all. In Jesus Christ's Name. Amen.

Beautiful and Godly Lady, are you ready to release all of the emotions that you have been harboring inside of you? Are you ready to move to another level in God? Are you ready to BE FREE to Be You? *21 Letters to a Beautiful and Godly Lady* shares with you the emotional highs and lows that we encounter in our lives. They are testimonies of the author's experiences and how God was able to release her through prayer, faith, and sometimes people. It's a

INTRODUCTION

journey of transparency and encouragement to assure every woman that they are a Beautiful and Godly Lady. Past mistakes, past hurts, and past failures are still beautiful to God. Let's go on this journey of spiritual freedom together and evolve even more to the Beautiful and Godly Lady our Father has birthed us to be.

ANGER

> *He that hath no rule over his own spirit is like a city that is broken down, and without walls.*
>
> — *PROVERBS 25:28*

Dear Beautiful and Godly Lady,

I once heard a quote that says, "he that angers you controls you." It wasn't until I got much older that I realized the anger I held inside was from the hurt, disappoint, and betrayal that I allowed to fester inside of my soul. Although my words say that I am not angry, my actions showed something different each time there was a trigger or a semblance of something remotely close to what I had experienced. My anger turned me into someone I did not know, I did not recognize, and most importantly someone I did not want to be. My anger distanced me from friendships and relationships because I held everyone accountable for that one moment of hurt, that one time of disappointment, that one person that betrayed me. Thankfully my anger did not result in me becoming physically aggressive. However, my words were just as deadly. The venom that spewed from my mouth when my anger erupted hurt people just as much as if they had been hit by a car. Then one day God revealed to me that the "he" that angers me is the devil. Satan's job is to kill, steal, and destroy every hope, dream, and purpose God has in store for me. Being honest, for quite some time I allowed him to do it. But not anymore. Anger hurt not only me; but it killed the spirit of love in everyone that was in my path. As I talk to you about it, it is reminding me of a song we use to sing as children. *"Sticks and stones may break my bones. But words will never hurt me."* There is no greater lie ever told. Words do hurt and not only do they hurt; but they leave an indelible impression that can never be erased. So many nights I have asked God's forgiveness for the angry words that I have lashed at others who did not deserve it. Thank God when I asked forgiveness from those I hurt, they forgave me. Beautiful and Godly Lady, release the spirit of anger. It is a bondage that holds you hostage and refuses to let you go. Allow God to rebuild, renew, and refresh every angry place in your heart and soul. Live a life that is free from torment and fury. Live a life that allows God to use you and make you whole. Beautiful and Godly Lady, when you release your anger you release every person connected including yourself. Release it and see.

Onward!

What is the source of your ANGER? How will you release it?

BE FREE. BE YOU.

ANXIETY

> *Do not be anxious about anything, but in every situation, by prayer and petition, with thanksgiving, present your requests to God.*
>
> — PHILIPPIANS 4:6 NIV

Dear Beautiful and Godly Lady,

I can write an entire book just on anxiety. This is an emotion that I am very familiar with it. Typically, my anxiety manifests when I have to speak publicly, or complete a project that includes working with other people. Oftentimes I experience anxiety when I have been promoted and it is time for me to lead others and I am not sure what that looks like. Do any of these situations sound familiar? The thoughts of what if I fail? What will they think of me? Am I not smart enough? Am I not pretty enough? I don't know what I am doing or what I am saying. It never fails that the very moment God graces me with an opportunity to represent Him is the very moment the devil steps in and counter attacks through thoughts, words, and other people. It took a lot of prayer and conversations with God to realize that the reason feelings (should be feelings) of anxiety overwhelms us is because we rely on our own abilities and talents instead of allowing the anointing of God to work through us. In life Beautiful and Godly Lady, we are groomed to be strong and self-sufficient. We are groomed to stand on our own and to excel in whatever we do. And in taking on self sufficiency and being strong in our own power, we create an anxiousness that says if we don't get it correct we have failed. I fully understand that anxiousness. I know the pressure of wanting everything you are involved in to be perfect. Doing the work yourself because everyone does not have your work ethic and whatever they return will not be completed in the attention to detail that you would have completed it can cause anxiety. Staying up late at night rehearsing your speech over and over again because every word has to be spoken articulately and you have to present yourself as being confident in what you are saying can also cause anxiety. Listen, I know because that "she" is me. The pressure I put on myself to have things completed in excellence developed into such an anxiety that I felt like I was going to have a break down. How did it get that way? It became that way because of expectation. The expectation of having to be perfect. The expectation of having to have it all together. The expectation of "if I don't do well it will be my last opportunity to do it again." The expectation of it all comes from your natural abilities and we dismiss God completely.

However, we were not taught that our strength comes from our Heavenly Father.

Philippians 4:6 teaches us to not be anxious about anything, but in every situation, by prayer and petition, with thanksgiving, present your requests to God.

Onward!

What causes you ANXIETY? How will you release your anxiety?

_____
_____
_____
_____
_____
_____
_____
_____
_____
_____
_____
_____
_____
_____
_____
_____
_____
_____
_____

BE FREE. BE YOU.

ROXANNE DIXON, ED.D

APOLOGIZING

> *Let us therefore follow after the things which make for peace, and things wherewith one may edify another.*
>
> — ROMANS 14:19

Dear Beautiful and Godly Lady,

I think one of the biggest breakthroughs that I have encountered in my life is the art of apologizing. Being able to say my apologies for the things I have said to you, the things I have done to you, and the things I have not done when you needed me. To make this art even greater is apologizing when you know that it was not your fault or even your intention; but apologizing because you know that God wants us to live in perfect peace.

Was this an easy process for me? Absolutely not! Was it the most liberating thing for me? Most definitely. I had come to a place where I wanted my life to be pleasing to God and to give Him the glory in everything that I do. I got into an argument with my husband over a difference of opinion and it escalated to a shouting match and storming out of the room vowing never to say anything to him again.

See, that is what I did. If I got into an argument with anyone my resolve was to walk away and promise myself that I would never speak to that person again. Thereby, I have my peace and they have their space and life is good. However, on that particular day, I was reading *Twelve Pillars* by Jim and Chris Widener while walking on the treadmill and a chapter came up entitled "All Communication Brings the Common Ground of Understanding." There was a quote in the book that recited *Communication is two or more people working together to find the common ground of understanding and when they find that common ground, they are positioned to have tremendous power together.* I had to ask myself were my husband and I having tremendous power together or were we becoming powerless. I then had an overwhelming compulsion to go and pray. As I prayed God spoke to me and said "go apologize." It was not about who was right; but it was about what was right. The only right thing is always giving God the glory. Arguing, disagreeing, holding grudges does not give God any glory.

Beautiful and Godly Lady, the bible teaches us in Romans 14:19 *Let us therefore follow after the things which make for peace, and things wherewith one may edify another.* Let go of things that hinder our peace and grasp those things that give us joy. Apologize to those that you have held hostage in your heart; even if that person is yourself.

Onward!

BE FREE. BE YOU.

Who do you need to APOLOGIZE to?

_____
_____
_____
_____
_____
_____
_____
_____
_____
_____
_____
_____
_____
_____
_____
_____
_____
_____
_____
_____
_____

BE FREE. BE YOU.

BAGGAGE

> Come to me, all you who are weary and burdened, and I will give you rest.
>
> — MATTHEW 11:28 NIV

Dear Beautiful and Godly Lady,

Growing up in New Orleans, it was normal to see homeless people walking everywhere. It was a part of our culture. We were taught to respect them because we did not know their situation or what led them to their circumstances. However, there was this one homeless lady that always stuck out in my mind. I would see her every day as I rode the bus to school. Regardless of the weather she wore this tattered coat and had this scarf covering her head. She would push this shopping cart and inside the cart she had bags on top of bags. I often wondered if that was everything she owned in those bags or was that everything she accumulated over the years inside those bags. Still to this day, I can vividly see this dear soul pushing her shopping cart of bags in the streets of New Orleans whether it was rain, shine, sleet, or snow. Day after day her cart became fuller and her attempt to push it became even harder.

Now that I am older, I still ponder whether those bags she carried were all of her possessions or was it the rubbish that she picked up over the years and added to her cart each day. Truth be told, we are symbolic of the homeless lady walking the streets of New Orleans. Yes, we have a domicile to reside in and no we don't push a shopping cart; but we do stockpile a myriad of baggage internally. Day after day we hold on to old wounds, old hurts, old memories that makes it harder for us to push forward every day. We carry scars that make us feel ashamed or we think we will be judged if people knew what happened to us. So instead of pushing a shopping cart like our homeless friend, we mask our carrier in Louis Vuitton bags, Coach bags, or Gucci bags. No one sees through our Chanel and Fendi outfits because on the outside we are well put together. Yet, on the inside we are a replica of the homeless lady with the tattered coat and the scarf covering her head pushing all the baggage that we have stored up for years. We cry at night when we are alone or in the shower where no one can hear us. We put on a smile in front of people because we have to show strength and courage but on the inside, we are crying for help. Those internal bags are getting heavier and heavier and we know we need help; but our pride won't allow us to ask. So, we go through life living a façade of who we have grown to be and never who God purposed us to be.

In John 5:6 Jesus asks the question *will thou be made whole*. In other words, do you want to live a perpetual life of being weighed down, burdened, and heavy ladened? Beautiful and Godly Lady, I did not want to be and you don't have to be. God tells us to come to him and He will give us rest. The baggage we carry can be released, if we want to release it. He wants us to cast our cares unto Him because He cares for us. I know what it feels like to carry the weight of heaviness but I also know what it feels like to release all to God and be free. No, it won't be easy because we have carried this baggage so long it has become a part of who we are. But the beauty of God is He knows how to make us whole. In Matthew 11:28 we are promised *Come to me, all you who are weary and burdened, and I will give you rest.* God always exchanges us beauty for our ashes. Trust me Beautiful and Godly Lady, it's okay to let go of your baggage. There is something greater waiting for you. Just let go and let God. It's worth the try.

Onward!

BE FREE. BE YOU.

What is the BAGGAGE you carry? How will you release your baggage?

BE FREE. BE YOU.

COMPARISON

> *Am I now trying to win the approval of human beings, or of God? Or am I trying to please people? If I were still trying to please people, I would not be a servant of Christ.*
>
> — GALATIANS 1:10 NIV

Dear Beautiful and Godly Lady,

Who are you comparing yourself to? "Am I built like her? Am I smart like her? Will he choose her over me? Why can't I be slimmer? Why can't I be bigger?" Sound familiar? I remember having a close friend that had a very complimentary shape. Hers was the kind of shape that would attract attention where ever she went. Me on the other hand, I was proportioned very well; however, I was more conservative with my attire and you could not distinguish whether I was a stick figure or coke bottle. Every time my friend and I would go out she was constantly attracting attention while I was on the sideline waiting for the novelty to wear off and we could continue with our evening. I must admit, the more attention she received the more I begin to look at myself and ask the questions "why isn't anyone looking at me?" "Why don't I dress like that?" "Why can't I be the center of attention?" Yes, the spirit of comparison was beginning to infiltrate my thinking and my spirit was opening a door to invite his friends jealously and envy in. One night as I was sitting in the car waiting for my friend, again, God spoke to me and said *what is seen is temporary but what is not seen is eternal* (2 Corinthians 4:8). He said while they are lusting on what is on the outside, they are missing the true treasure of what you have on the inside. Beautiful and Godly Lady the only comparison you have is to yourself. God told us that we are uniquely and wonderfully made. So what if we don't have what someone else has? But what God has given us is just enough. God wants us to love who we are because He did not make a mistake. He promised us in Jeremiah 29 that He has plans for us and He will bring us to an expected end. Challenge yourself to be the best you that you can be. Release yourself from comparing yourself to others. God has graced, gifted, and guaranteed that He has created us to be everything we need to be and that is enough.

Onward!

Who are you comparing yourself to? How will you release the spirit of COMPARISON?

BE FREE. BE YOU.

COURAGE

> *Be strong and courageous. Do not be afraid or terrified because of them, for the LORD your God goes with you; he will never leave you nor forsake you.*
>
> — DEUTERONOMY 31:6 NIV

Dear Beautiful and Godly Lady,

I had the wonderful experience of growing up during a time when we loved to go outside and play. We could not wait to get home from school and indulge in a game of football, or a pickup game of basketball. When we got tired of playing with the boys, we would play 1-2-3 red light or Mother May I. We loved going from game to game; but nothing was more tantalizing than when one of our friends came outside with an extremely long phone cord that we affectionately called our "rope." Now if you were a novice, you played regular rope; but if you were an experienced jumper like me you got to play with the older girls in a complicated rope game named "Double Dutch." See, Double Dutch is different from regular jump rope because there are two ropes. The two people must be skilled in turning because the ropes have to be synchronized in order for them to be evenly turned. Thinking back to those days, it's playing Double Dutch that is similar to the way we look at life. Let's look at life like those two ropes... As each rope turns, we will say that it's another year of our life turning. Now, it's our turn to jump in the rope. We posture ourselves to jump in by standing at the end and with each turn we anticipate our entrance into the rope. With anticipation, thoughts flood our minds like..."Can't jump in because you're going too fast...you're going to slow...it's not the right time...I don't know how to do it...If I mess up they will laugh at me...nobody taught me how to do this." Bad enough you are nervous to jump in; but to make matters worse, sometimes you have people waiting behind you, yelling "hurry up, you don't know how to jump, you are taking too long, get out the way."

Then with all the strength you can muster, finally you jump in and you make it one or two turns but your foot or head or hand gets caught in the rope and you get tangled up. But what do you do? You untangle yourself and get up and try again with a promise that the next time you will jump longer and with each go round you get better and better.

Beautiful and Godly Lady jump in the rope of life and enjoy it. The first time you may stumble and get tangled but get up and do it again and again and again.

Deuteronomy 31:6 (NIV) says: *Be strong and courageous. Do not be afraid or terrified because of them, for the LORD your God goes with you; he will never leave you nor forsake you.* Don't live life like the girls who are turning the rope; always watching someone else jump in but never attempting to try themselves. Like the constant movement of the rope turning, life if constantly turning and every day you are anticipating jumping in is another day of opportunity you miss. The world is waiting for you to make your move. JUMP! You will be just fine.

Onward!

What desire do you have? How will you release COURAGE to get it done?

BE FREE. BE YOU.

DELAYS

> *But they that wait upon the Lord shall renew their strength; they shall mount up with wings as eagles; they shall run, and not be weary; and they shall walk, and not faint.*
>
> — *ISAIAH 40:3*

Dear Beautiful and Godly Lady,

I tell my husband all the time I live a delayed by not a denied life. You are probably wondering what I mean by that. I may be the only one, but it seems like things I desire often takes a longer time to happen than other people. Not comparing myself to anyone; however, I look at people and see them being blessed and am amazed at how quickly God moved in their lives. People being promoted, people getting married, people being elevated, people opening businesses, people writing books, people being financially blessed, people's marriages being restored, people's health being restored, people building friendships, people growing in God and I sit amazed but yet dumbfounded on how they got all these blessings. (Oh let's be transparent shall we) I look at people, especially those I've been around, and say Lord how in the world did you bless them before me? Father, I know you know what they did because I know what they did. Then I begin to have an entire dialogue with God about how I have done so many wonderful things compared to them, yet what I truly desire has not manifested and it doesn't look like it has even been thought about. It took me arriving at a place of spiritual maturity to realize that God shows no favoritism according to Romans 2:11NLT. I was trying to anthropomorphize God and hold him to an accountability that I would hold my mom or friends to. Then, secondly, God had to reveal to me that the blessing I saw manifesting in the life of someone else may not have come as immediately as I thought it did. What I saw was the manifestation of the blessing. God said you were not there to see the toiling, time, tenacity, and travail that they endured while praying to Me to bless them. He said you did not see the nights they stayed working long after they had gotten off from work, and put their family to sleep to work on their vision. Nor did you see the times they cried and were ready to give up because of the frustration and the feeling of having no one supporting them. God continued to say you weren't there when they prayed to me fervently because they knew this vision came from me, but they did not know where to begin or how to finance it. Lastly, you did not see how many times they had to start over because it did not work out the first time; but they were determined not to give up. There is a quote that says, "we see the glory; but we don't know the story." Then it all begins to make sense.

I am what's called a special order. My family and friends call me a picky eater because I like my food prepared a specific way. When we go out to eat I can't just order directly from the menu because there are certain sauces or condiments on the food that I don't particularly have a taste for. So, while everyone else places their order directly from the menu, I have to ask the waiter to listen carefully because I am going to give specific instructions on the way I would like my meal prepared. Each time I do this the waiter replies "this is a special order and will take a little bit longer to prepared." After a few minutes the waiter would bring everyone's food to the table; but my food would be delayed because the chef is preparing it especially for me. A little while later, the waiter returns to the table and says your special order is now ready. Like an inspector, I carefully check the intimate details of my meal to ensure it is exactly like I requested. And with delight I thank the waiter for ensuring my order was exactly what I wanted.

Beautiful and Godly Lady, we are special orders and our desires are special orders. God is taking His time to create for us exactly what we need. And in the midst of his creation, we must stay strong, stay committed, and wait the course. Isaiah 40:31 tells us *but they that wait upon the Lord shall renew their strength; they shall mount up with wings as eagles; they shall run, and not be weary; and they shall walk, and not faint.* Our only responsibility is to wait and not wait with anxiousness but wait with reassurance that God will deliver what he promised. God's promises to us are yea and amen. Therefore, our delay is not a denial. Our delay is our preparation time to get ready for the overflow of blessings that will be bestowed upon us. God is ordaining just the right season so that we won't miss it. In our delay Beautiful and Godly Lady, get ready. Our cries, our petition, our intercession is reaching the ears of God. Our delay is not a denial it is simply a special order that God is seasoning perfectly for us. Your time is coming, and it won't be long. Stay the course and keep the faith. I guarantee you it will be exactly what you ordered.

Onward!

What DELAYS are you waiting for? What can you be doing until the manifestation of your delays arrive?

_____
_____
_____
_____
_____
_____
_____
_____
_____
_____
_____
_____
_____
_____
_____
_____
_____
_____
_____
_____

DISAPPOINTMENT

> *Now thanks be unto God, who always causeth us to triumph in Christ and who maketh manifest through us the savour of His knowledge in every place.*
>
> — *2 CORINTHIANS 2:14*

Dear Beautiful and Godly Lady,

It is one thing to be disappointed when you do not receive something that you really wanted; like a promotion, a compliment, or your Amazon package to arrive a day earlier. That is one level of disappointment but it is another entire level of disappointment when you expect someone that is truly close to you like a family member, a spouse, or a really close friend to disappoint you. Oh I know it oh so well. The most hurtful thing about it is I went against my own principle and allowed them to enter my space. My heart. A place that I promised no one could enter because I have been disappointed so many times before. I truly understand what Psalm 55:12 means when it says *It is not an enemy who taunts me— I could bear that. It is not my foes who so arrogantly insult me— I could have hidden from them. Instead, it is you—my equal my companion and close friend.* As I matured through life, I learned that disappointment comes from our expectation of what we want a person to do or say or how to behave and it does not come from the act itself that the person did. The person did all that they knew to do. We have put our template, our desire, our hope, our expectation on what we desired of them only for them to respond in the only manner that they know how. Is that on them or is that on us? Allow me to give you an example. For years I have had the desire to do something creatively. It was impregnated in me by God and I carried it in my spirit for years and years. One day I decided, with the unction of the Holy Spirit, to go forth and birth the idea. With fear and trembling not knowing how it would work out, I said, "I will press forward and believe God for the outcome." But first, I wanted to share my upcoming baby with my close friend, confidant, and mentor. I shared my idea and what I thought would be a big congratulations turned into a disaster. After the conversation, I felt disappointed, hurt, and confused. The one thing that I asked for ever was shot down. So, what did I do? I put my baby back on the shelf and looked at it from a distance. What should I have done? I should have pressed forward. Why? Because I stated previously God gave it to me. Beautiful and Godly Lady, our disappointments come because we rely on the approval of man. Yes and absolutely we must remain under authority and do everything in decency and order. However, when God gives you instructions, He is the ultimate authority. When God says, "move" there is no need for approval. God has the final say and in between God's yea and amen. He has already provided the provisions, resources, and approval needed to press forward. 2 Corinthians 2:14 reminds us *now thanks be unto God, who always causeth us to triumph in Christ and who maketh manifest through us the savor of His knowledge in every place.* Don't allow disappointment to hold you hostage. What God has for us is for us and He constantly opens doors that no man can shut, and shuts doors that no man can open. Release disappointment today and seek God for guidance. And if that is not enough, let us never forget that one day in this life we disappointed someone and through God's grace and mercy they forgave us. You got this.

Onward!

Who are, or what DISAPPOINTED you? How will you release disappointment?

BE FREE. BE YOU.

DOUBT

> *And whatever you do, whether in word or deed, do it all in the name of the Lord Jesus, giving thanks to God the Father through him.*
>
> — *COLOSSIANS 3:17NIV*

Dear Beautiful and Godly Lady,

There are so many opportunities that I have missed out on because I doubted myself. I didn't think I knew all the information or I felt like people would laugh at me. In my head I conjured thoughts of failing or no one caring. Even writing this book, I am doubting myself saying no one wants to hear about my experiences. Can I be honest? Even in my Christian journey, knowing all the scriptures in the bible, I still have doubt. What I had to learn is that doubt and fear are cousins. If one does not stop you the other one will try. But, what we have to do is stand firm knowing that if we trust in God our paths will be directed.

Every time I doubt myself, God has to remind me that it is not about me it is about Him. Colossians 3:17 asserts that whatever we do in word or deed that we should be doing for the Lord. Our doubt manifests when we take God out of the equation and rely on ourselves. When we think our natural gifts and talents will suffice and we become hubristic being falsely assured that it is solely on us forgetting that it is He that made us and not we ourselves. The doubt we feel is a reminder that this is not about us but it is about giving glory and honor to God. Beautiful and Godly Lady, God promised that before we were born He knew what we would be. We can only be who God called us to be if we keep God in the equation. Whenever you are feeling doubtful invite God into the moment. Allow Him to direct and instruct you as to what to do. Open your heart to the leading and guiding of the Holy Spirit. When we don't know what to do He does.

Onward!

BE FREE. BE YOU.

How will you release DOUBT?

BE FREE. BE YOU.

ENEMIES

> Ye did run well; who did hinder you that ye should not obey the truth?
>
> — GALATIANS 5:7

Dear Beautiful and Godly Lady,

I have always been pretty popular. Regardless of the setting I have been genuinely liked and accepted. Fortunately, I have not experienced enemies personally; however, I do know that all of us have some somewhere in this world. But, those are not the enemies I want to discuss in this letter. The enemy I want to discuss in this letter is the enemy that stops us from doing our best. The enemy causes us to retreat when we want to fight. The enemy tells us we can't do something because we aren't good enough or smart enough or pretty enough. Yes, I know that I said I have never experienced an enemy; but maybe that wasn't the total truth. I have experienced an enemy. No, not the enemy disguised as friends or families that secretly desire to have what you have. No, not the enemy that believes you have wronged them and is secretly plotting revenge against you. The greatest enemy that I had to come face to face with was my "*inner me.*" My *inner me* had a voice of influence that was so much louder than any person could ever have. My inner me shot down every idea I dreamed of. My inner me challenged every move I decided to make. My inner me had me questioning my own judgement. My inner me was supposed to be my biggest cheerleader and my number one encourager. However, somewhere along the line my inner me connected with the worst part of me and decided to betray me. Yes, it was easy for me to blame other people for my shortcomings by saying you don't support me or you don't believe me. The reality of it all was my inner me holding me hostage to the hurts, scars, and pains of my past. My inner me was building a so-called safety net for me not to get hurt while all along it was a cage to keep me confined to a life of mediocrity. Galatians 5:7 asks the question *Ye did run well; who did hinder you that ye should not obey the truth?* When we were younger our dreams were as wide as the ocean. We envisioned as far as our imagination would take us. Beautiful and Godly Lady, it is time to dream again. It is time to release the enemy of your inner me and walk in your destiny. Everyone is waiting for you to let your light shine. The world needs what you have to offer. It is not too late.

Onward!

How will you release ENEMIES?

BE FREE. BE YOU.

FAILURE

 For as he thinketh in his heart, so is he.

— PROVERBS 23:7

Dear Beautiful and Godly Lady,

Somewhere along in life, I put his high demand on myself to achieve and accomplish at the highest level, whatever I put my hand to do. If I am responsible for it, I put this unreachable expectation that if it is not perfect I have failed, not realizing that failure is not a bad thing. Failure can be a good thing if you fail forward. The year before last, I worked diligently and earnestly to get my school to a high level of instruction. It was my goal to make sure that the teachers, students, and superiors see that regardless of the demographics of my school, we could accomplish a high level of achievement. Day after day, fight after fight, cry after cry my staff and I worked overtime with the hopes and prayers that this would be the year of our breakthrough. The time came for our students to test and show the world that we were a force to be reckoned with. The day finally came and I can remember it like I was still in that day. I received a text saying, "check your portal the scores are in." With excitement and some fear I was ready. I was ready to see the fruits of our labor and broadcast it from the highest mountain. I opened my portal, searched for my school, and located my scores. At the moment my eyes met with the score my heart leaped. Could this be true? Could this be accurate? Could this even be possibly possible? My school's score was a 6! Yes, a 6! Not a 6 out of 7 or even a 6 out of 10; but a 6 out of 100! What happened? What occurred? Why me? Without provocation and in front of all of my leaders I cried...the ugly cry. For me I felt I failed. I failed myself, I failed my staff, I failed my school, I failed my parents. You name them and I felt like I failed them. Immediately my thoughts were consumed with failure, and when my thoughts became consumed with failure my actions began to represent failure. My stress level increased. My joy went away. I started looking for a new job. Then one day, while operating in my spirit of failure, God had to reveal some things to me. Firstly, God said you are not defined by one score. All the great things that have been put in place at your school can not be identified by a score. Secondly, you are the only one that sees you as a failure. So get out of yourself. It's not about you. Did you even consider me and where I am in all of this? And finally, you are my child and I always cause you to triumph. I am in the midst of all of this, you just have to trust me even when you can't trace me. Beautiful and Godly Lady, often times we measure our success and failure by a barometer of tangible things. Our success and failures are not defined by what we can put our hands on. 2 Corinthians 4:18 teaches us *While we look not at the things which are seen, but at the things which are not seen: for the things which are seen are temporal; but the things which are not seen are eternal.* We should define our successes and failures by the souls we win for the kingdom and the opportunities to share Christ with others. Everything will not happen the way we want it to or how we want it to; but instead of counting it as a failure, see God in the midst of it. At that moment He may not be obvious; but keep looking He is there.

Onward!

How will you release FAILURE?

_____
_____
_____
_____
_____
_____
_____
_____
_____
_____
_____
_____
_____
_____
_____
_____
_____
_____
_____

BE FREE. BE YOU.

FAITH

 For we walk by faith, not by sight.

— 2 CORINTHIANS 5:7

Dear Beautiful and Godly Lady,

When I desired to become an Administrator, in the natural the odds were stacked against me; but in the spiritual I knew God had a plan for my life. I mean after all God promised me that He would bring me to an expected end and I believed Him. I didn't have the years of experience. I didn't have the connections. I didn't have the relationships with the new administration, and I didn't have the support of some of my colleagues. But the one thing I did have was FAITH! All my life, I followed the rules as prescribed. Go to school, go to college, do your best on your job, operate in the position that you want, not the one that you currently have. I did. Admittedly, I went far and beyond on my job. I went early and stayed late. I started new programs, and trained new people. I read every leadership book there was and I can confess I was recognized for my accomplishments. However, to get ready to move to such a higher position, for me, took a lot more than my gifts and talents could offer. There were so many people that had much more experience, accomplished more, led their teams to championships and then there was me. I was just starting out of the gate. I had never led anything independently, let alone an entire building and a community that would look to me for answers and leadership. Whew, this was way out of my comfort zone. But the one thing I had was faith. And in my faith I knew I could trust God to lead me and tell me if it was the right time. So, I stepped out on faith and applied. I applied for something that was greater than my abilities...at the time.

At the time of the interviews my church was on a fast and my Bishop instructed us to write down what we needed God to do. So I did. I fasted. I prayed. I wanted the position so badly, my husband and I would go to the building, after church, and pray in front of it. I studied the organization inside and out. I researched the community. I asked people that had a relationship with God to touch and agree with me and silenced those that tried to talk against my desire. This faith walk was different for me. It was different because I could not control the outcome. It was different because throughout the process I had to be conscious not to allow fear to overtake me as I went to interviews with the leaders of the organization. It was different because I had to be meticulous in the words, I spoke about how I was progressing through the process. I needed God more than ever because I did not know what I was doing; but he did. I remember finishing one of the interviews and a friend called to see how I made out. After sharing the details of what happened he gave me this advice. He said in the book of Esther Chapter Two the story tells of (remove "of") how Esther was preparing to go to see the king. As the story goes there were other young ladies prior to Esther that had the same opportunity to see the king; however, when it was Esther's turn in Esther 2:15 the scripture says *Esther obtained favour in the sight of all them that looked upon her.* My friend said from here to the end of your process say to yourself, "I am Esther (Roxanne) and I have favor in the sight of all those that look upon me." Guess what? I did. From the community to the top person in the organization, before entering any meeting or any interview I said to myself, "I am Roxanne and I have favor in the sight of all those that look upon me." Beautiful and Godly Lady, what I said mattered and having the faith to believe in what I said mattered even more. 2 Corinthians 5:7 reminds us *for we walk by faith, not by sight*. In my eyes every card was stacked against me; but in my faith I knew if God be for me, who could be against me. That entire process was a faith walk. I leaned and depended on God the entire way and ultimately I was offered the position. Beautiful and Godly Lady, I challenge you to exercise your faith muscle to do something that is beyond your own abilities to do. Challenge your faith to create opportunities that are bigger than your skills and abilities. See beyond what you can see and allow God to expand your vision. Have faith to know that what God has for you is for you. And if He allows you to have it, you are well equipped to handle it. Take a leap of faith and see where you land. It is worth the risk. I promise. See you on the other side.

Onward!

How will you release FAITH?

BE FREE. BE YOU.

FEAR

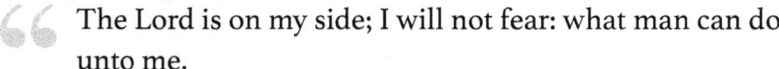

> " The Lord is on my side; I will not fear: what man can do unto me.
>
> — PSALM 118:6

Dear Beautiful and Godly Lady,

 know fear too well. Fear of failing. Fear of trying something new. Fear of not being accepted. Fear of being laughed at. Fear of stepping out on your faith. Fear of opening your business. Fear of writing this book. My list can go on and on. I'm sure your list can go on as well. However, one day I had to sit and reflect: where did the root of my fear generate? What was the genesis of this fear that I carried around like my purse? I could say it came from my upbringing in a form of protection by my mom or I can say it came from hearing the failures that surrounded me or I can even say it was perpetuated by the scripture Galatians 5:7 that says *Ye did run well; who did hinder you that ye should not obey the truth?* I would love to blame so many people and so many things on why I had become so fearful; but the truth of the matter is, I was the one to blame. I

allowed myself to stop me from trying something new. I allowed myself to stop me from stepping out on faith. I was afraid of the unknown, conjuring thoughts in my own head of what if it doesn't work, or what if I don't succeed, or what if I f...a...i...l? The truth of the matter is what if I do succeed? What if they do accept me? What if they don't laugh at me? How about what if they do? Who are these "they's" and why do matter? The" they's" are the imaginary people that we conjure up in our own thoughts that continue to stop us from living our purpose. The "they's" are the ideas that we allow Satan to plant in our minds to keep us focused on what we can't do instead of what we can do. Fear is a direct attack from the dart of Satan that he shoots aimlessly. He does not care where it hits as long as it hits and wounds our creativity, our genius, and our passion. God promised us in Jeremiah 29:11 that He *had a plan for our life and that plan was is to prosper us and bring us to an expected end.* Holding on to that promise, our only responsibility is to operate in the purpose that God has called us to, and the outcome is left up to God. We get so focused on how the outcome will turn out that we lose sight of the entire purpose.

Beautiful and Godly Lady, time is moving swiftly. Write your book. Open your business. Start your ministry. Go back to school. If God gave you a vision then He will provide provision for the manifestation. Don't allow fear to stifle, paralyze, or delay what God has already anointed to prosper. Walk in your gifts and talents. Walk in your anointing. Walk in your calling. There are millions of people waiting for you to release what God has birthed inside of you. There are millions of people anticipating the delivery of your blessing. And most of all God is waiting for you to give Him the glory by following His instructions and doing what He has called you to do. Be fearless. God is with us and we shall not fail.

Onward!

How will you release FEAR?

BE FREE. BE YOU.

KINDNESS

> *Don't forget to show hospitality to strangers, for some who have done this have entertained angels without realizing it!*
>
> — *HEBREWS 13:2 (NLT)*

Dear Beautiful and Godly Lady,

God granted me the most beautiful experience. I had the opportunity to meet an angel and did not know it. When I arrived in Atlanta due to Hurricane Katrina, let's just say my money was funny and my change was strange. I did not have a job at the moment nor did I have residency. All my daughter and I had was the kindness of strangers because we had no family in Atlanta and only knew one other person. Then one day, God sent us an angel. We heard that the local post office was offering free P.O. boxes for Katrina evacuees. Not having a residence and trying to get established, we thought it would be a good idea to secure a P.O. Box to have somewhere to receive mail. Unbeknownst to us that when it was our turn to speak to the cashier she belligerently exclaimed there were no free P.O. Boxes and if we wanted one we would have to pay like everyone else. Embarrassed of course, we attempted to plead with her our situation; but to no avail. With the post office crowded and us holding up the line, out of nowhere a voice came from the back of the line saying "I'll pay for their box!" Turning around to see who made the offer; to our surprise it was a statuesque older lady wearing a local county's police uniform. Trying to remain humble but yet grateful, we graciously declined the offer; but the young lady was not having it. She made her way to the front of the line and paid for our P.O. Box, not just for a month; but for an entire year. Needless to say, we were so grateful and thankful to the stranger we could not stop saying thank you. After making the transaction, we adjourned outside to introduce ourselves and make small talk; thinking that was the end of our blessing. Who knew that it was just the beginning? Not taking no for an answer, the officer treated us to lunch at one of her favorite restaurants. She introduced us to all of the staff and made it known that we were relocating due to Hurricane Katrina and were now her new friends. Wanting to ensure that we had all the necessities, the Officer asked where were we banking. Being new we had not thought that far, so she insisted on taking us to her local bank to open an account. When we arrived at the bank, she introduced us to the tellers and loan officers. The loan officer walked us into the office to begin the process of opening an account. I remember it so clearly she asked me "do you have one dollar to open an account with?" My reply was "yes, we have a dollar." But before, I could finish our friend, the Officer, interjected and said "I will put money in their account. I was going to buy food for my horses; but I can use it for this instead." Without hesitation, the Officer, transferred five hundred dollars into our new bank account. We were floored, confused, amazed, happy, (add "and a bit")skeptical; but yet, at the same time, grateful. See, just the day before, I was offered a teaching position and my daughter was enrolled in school. I had no money to purchase work clothes let alone school uniforms. That five hundred dollars was exactly what we needed to get us up and running. Now, back to the story. After that day, the Officer stayed in contact with me, assisting me with finding an apartment, and checking to make sure we were okay until we became established and were on our feet. Thereafter, our communication became minimal to almost non-existent. A year rolled around and we had made our residency in Atlanta. We didn't need that P.O. Box anymore; I was secure at work, and my daughter was thriving in school. It was the holidays and my daughter and I decided to invite the Officer over to show our appreciation and bless her like she blessed us. With eagerness, I dialed her phone number excited to extend an invitation only to be greeted by an operator telling me that her number was no longer in service. Hmm, that was strange; but no worries because I knew where she worked. She wasn't just any officer. She was an officer working in the K-9 unit. Looking up the number, I contacted the local police office, specifically the K-9 unit, and asked for her. The officer on the other end of the phone explained to me that there was no officer there by that name. I argued with him that he was wrong. I know her name, I saw her police car, I even saw her dog. With fervor, he said it over and over again that she did not work there and never did. We were determined not to give up so we went back to the local restaurant and asked had she come back in and were told they had not seen her since the day she was with us. Surely, she had to have gone back to the bank. She still needed money to live. So, we went back to the bank and spoke with the loan officer that assisted us and she said the same thing everyone else said *I have not seen her since the day she came in with you.* We were perplexed, puzzled, and outright confused...what was happening? Then I realized, God sent us an angel. In our time of need God knew exactly what we needed. It was the kindness of a stranger that assisted on our journey. We were in a foreign land with foreign people and God sent us help through a stranger's kindness to show us that everything was going to be alright.

 Beautiful and Godly Lady, I have heard the saying before "kindness goes a long way" and I can attest to the fact that the kindness of that Officer, through the power and an anointing of God, opened doors for us that could not be closed and closed door for us that could not be open. The beauty of it all was she was of a different hue, she was not familiar to the company we usually keep, and she was a servant of God doing His will for His people. Let kindness lead you

Beautiful and Godly Lady. Whether you are receiving kindness or you are extending kindness, allow it to be infectious and contagious because you do not know the blessing that it has behind it. From that experience until now, God has blessed me exceedingly abundantly and it all started from the kindness of a stranger saying *I'll pay for it*. Let's see what our kindness can do for someone else and see how far it will go.

Onward!

BE FREE. BE YOU.

How will you release KINDNESS?

BE FREE. BE YOU.

OBEDIENCE

 Behold, to obey is better than sacrifice.

— 1 SAMUEL 15:22

Dear Beautiful and Godly Lady,

Would you believe me if I told you a cake saved my life? Well it did. In my B.C. days...Before Christ. We have all had those times before we accepted Christ as our personal Lord and Savior. I shamefully admit that I was not the nicest person to certain people. I was very brusque and rude; sometimes disrespectful and not kind with my words. Thank God for Jesus. Unfortunately, this distasteful behavior was exercised on a young lady that I worked with daily. The young lady was saved and filled with the Holy Spirit and I on the other hand was filled with my own self-righteousness and self-inflated ego. Every night we reported to work I made it my mission to do something that would take the young lady out of her spiritual element and move her to my dark side. And every night the young would counter act my behavior by spewing scriptures at me or trying to anoint my head with oil. This daily cat and mouse game became entertainment for me, so each day I would think of something outlandish to do to irritate or vex her spirit. Thankfully nothing worked and the young lady stood on her beliefs. I would say this back and forth banter went on for probably about three months and then my birthday rolled around. I made it to another year older; life was good as I deemed it to be, and off to work I went ready to pursue my pleasure like Wile E. Coyote and the Road Runner. When I entered the room, there was a birthday cake on the table and the inscription read "Happy Birthday Roxanne." Shocked and amazed, I inquired who bought me this cake. The other employees, thoroughly amused, proclaimed it was from the young lady that I had purposely harassed for the last three months. In that moment something came over me and I had to sit quietly for a minute. I stared at the cake in amazement. No, it was not the beauty of the physical cake; but it was the beauty of the message behind the cake and that message resounded loud and clear in my spirit. It was so loud that these words came out of my mouth, "If you can buy me a cake after all the things I have done to you, I want to know the God that you serve." I was having my own Saul to Paul on the road to Damascus experience. It was that day that I began my journey of salvation. That is not the end of the story. Years later I was able to reconnect with the young lady through email. I was excited to share with her my spiritual transformation and how I am now winning souls for Christ. Her response to my email was more than I expected. She said "Dear Roxanne, It is great to hear from you and I am happy to hear that you are on your spiritual journey. You don't know the struggle I had to purchase you that cake that day. All through church I wrestled with God about buying it for you. It wasn't until I was almost at work that I decided to be obedient and follow God's instructions. I don't know who life that cake saved that day; yours or mine?"

Beautiful and Godly Lady, what if she had not been obedient? What if she had not followed God's instructions? Our obedience is often times not about us but for the salvation of someone else's soul. And often times those people are not the kindest people to us. Yes, they were mean to us. Yes, they said some unkind words. Yes, they hurt us. But, didn't they do the same to Jesus. Better yet, didn't we do the same to Jesus? The Bible teaches us in 1 Samuel 15:22 *obedience is better than sacrifice*. We must obey the instructions given by God so that we are not sacrificing the souls, lives, gifts, and talents of not just ourselves but also of other people. I told you a cake saved my life.

Onward!

BE FREE. BE YOU.

How will you release OBEDIENCE?

BE FREE. BE YOU.

OBSTACLES

> For I can do all things through Christ who gives me strength.
>
> — PHILIPPIANS 4:13 NLT

Dear Beautiful and Godly Lady,

Recently I started really getting into health and fitness. One of the things I decided to do was to get up early every morning and walk my cul-de-sac. I saw my neighbors walking and I thought what better way to explore my neighborhood, get some fresh air, and get fit at the same time. Little did I know that the streets of my neighborhood were laced with deep inclines. WHEW! Wait, before I even get to the street I have to walk the deepest incline of them all...my drive way. Sharing a transparent moment, the first time I walked up the drive way to get to the street I was so out of breath that it deterred me and I turned right around and went back in the house. It was at that moment that I realized I had to do something different. I had to think different. The quote *if you want something different you have to do something different* kept playing in my head. So, I decided that I would not let that drive way defeat me. The next morning I awoke, with determination to make it to the street. I tackled the drive way. Now, I did have to stand there for a moment so I could breathe before I was able to walk. Nonetheless, I made it. Being proud of myself, I began my journey of fitness and started walking. Unbeknownst to me, my street felt like it was built on top of Stone Mountain. Every 200 feet was an incline. I could not get momentum because every time I did I approached another incline! It was an obstacle! Webster defines obstacle as a thing that blocks one's way or prevents or hinders progress. I could not allow these obstacles to stop me. My health is too important. My mind is too important. My well-being is too important. So what did I do? I named every incline I approached. Because I became familiar with their locations, I knew when I was about to approach them so I prepared myself. I told myself Philippians 4:13 *for I can do all things through Christ who gives me strength.* As I approached the first obstacle, I named it "fear" and said, "fear you will not stop me." Guess what? I made it over. I named the second obstacle "anxiety." I told the second obstacle the same thing "anxiety, you will not stop me." Guess what? I made it over that one too. Each obstacle I approached I named it and I challenged myself to get over it. Then one day, I realized that I had not exerted as much energy to get over the incline. I wasn't as out of breath. Each incline was getting easier and I began to look for steeper inclines because I told myself if I got over the first set of inclines than surely I can master the second set.

Beautiful and Godly Lady, don't allow the inclines of life stop you from reaching your goal. God has equipped each and every one of us with the skills and talents to maximize every purpose He has put inside of us. Build your tenacity. Build your resilience. Stand on your faith in knowing who you are and whose you are. Name your inclines and meet them head on. The reward is so much greater on the other side. All we have to do is pursue it. God is with us; we will not fail.

Onward!

How will you release OBSTACLES?

_____
_____
_____
_____
_____
_____
_____
_____
_____
_____
_____
_____
_____
_____
_____
_____
_____
_____

BE FREE. BE YOU.

PERSERVERANCE

> *And I am sure of this, that he who began a good work in you will bring it to completion at the day of Jesus Christ.*
>
> — *PHILIPPIANS 1:6 ESV*

Dear Beautiful and Godly Lady,

One weekend my husband and I decided to take a drive to Alabama. It was during the COVID-19 quarantine time and we both had cabin fever. Taking long drives are our favorite thing to do together, so we decided why not. We especially love to look at the view of the mountains and watch in awe of God's masterpiece and picturesque landscaping. It was a nice clear sunny day, so we had the sunroof open so the sun could shine through and we could look up, see the clear skies, and fluffy clouds. Enjoying the ride and engaging in great conversations, we noticed that as we drove our clear skies were beginning to become a little cloudy and overcast; but nonetheless, we continued our journey enjoying the view. We noticed the further we traveled the darker the sky became. The further we traveled the darker the clouds became. The further we traveled our once beautiful scenery became more difficult to see. If the darkness was not bad enough, we began to feel rain come through the sunroof. It was not enough rain to close the sunroof; but enough to get our attention. As we drove further, what was once a little drizzle had now turned into a down pour mixed with hail. At this point we had no other choice but to close the sunroof, turn on the windshield wipers, grasp the steering wheel, and hold on tight. We were on the highway, our vision was obscured, but we never thought to pull over because we asked God to cover us as we continued on our journey. As we drove, I looked ahead and what I saw arrested my attention. Although we were pounded by hail, rain was pouring down, our visibility was limited, and the sky was as black as the night; on the other side of the mountain I could see that the sun was still shining. Due to the inclement weather, we had to reduce our speed and our trip arrival time was extended. It didn't matter because we knew if we kept going, we were going to meet the sun on the other side of the mountain.

Beautiful and Godly Lady, isn't that story just like life? Sometimes we are in the midst of the greatest time of our lives. Everything is going in our favor. We are happy, we are prosperous, we are operating in our gifts and talents, we moving and shaking, and then one day a cloud of disappointment shows up. Then another cloud of bad news follows. From there a hail storm of rejection, financial struggles, pandemics, marital issues, health issues, and the list goes on and on overwhelms you. Be encouraged! Just as we kept driving, Beautiful and Godly Lady keep moving. The sun is shining on the other side of your adversities. Don't stop! Don't give up. In the midst of our ride, we saw a lot of cars that decided to pull over or get off at an exit that wasn't theirs. If only they would have kept going. You are at the periphery of your breakthrough and manifestation if you would just keep going. Yes, you may have to refocus. Yes, you may have to readjust. Yes, you may have to replace, reassign, or even reestablish some things in your life; but don't stop. Not only is the S-U-N shining on the other side of your dark days; but the S-O-N is directing our path through it all. Philippians 1:6 affirms that *And I am sure of this, that he who began a good work in you will bring it to completion at the day of Jesus Christ I assure you that you will arrive at your destination because God has promised us an expected end.* Keep moving! You will get there.

Onward!

What are some things that have stopped you from your PERSERVERANCE? How will you keep moving?

___

BE FREE. BE YOU.

QUITTING

> *Let us not become weary in doing good, for at the proper time we will reap a harvest if we do not give up.*
>
> — *GALATIANS 6:9 NIV*

Dear Beautiful and Godly Lady,

hen we were younger, my mother always believed that an idle mind is the devil's workshop. Therefore, we were never allowed to have free time. If we were not in school my siblings and I were constantly engaged in some sort of afterschool activity, church vacation bible school, park recreation, or club. Being the baby of the family and a form of tom boy thanks to my older brother, you could usually find me outside engaged in playing football with the neighborhood kids, basketball, cheerleading, or jumping rope. You name it. Well, this one time I decided to stretch myself and run track at the neighborhood park. Having no formal track experience I thought, "how hard could it be?" So, I gathered my not made for running sneakers and headed to the neighborhood recreation center and introduced myself to the track coach and informed him that I wanted to be on the team. He gave me a look over and said okay. Hey, we weren't practicing for the Olympics so it was a whosoever type of deal. Every day after school I would go to the park and practice. Every day Coach would have me run around the track, pushing me more and more daily. His words to me were, "take your time in the first lap, build your momentum, and give it all you have at the end. Everyone leaves the gate running as fast as they can but by the second lap they become tired and can't make it to the end." I kept that advice in my runners' tool belt. I did not know exactly when I would use it; but hey it was there. One day I came to practice to be greeted by Coach informing me that the upcoming Saturday we would have a track meet. Every nerve in my body seemed like it fell in my stomach as I became instantly ill. Of course Coach assured me that I had nothing to worry about if I remembered the advice he had given me. Saturday, the big race arrived. The stands were saturated with people; including my mother and brothers. The announcer announced our names and we all took our position. The gun fired and we were off. As coach predicted the young ladies took off like a bolt of lightning. Exerting all of their energy they were determined to win the race. Me on the other hand I started off at a very slow pace. Constantly reminding myself of what Coach said I focused my attention on my lane and ran at a decent speed. I could hear from the side the people in the stands laughing and out of the corner of my eye I could also see them pointing at me, including my brothers. Not allowing it to deter me, I continued to run keeping the other young ladies in my sight. As I rounded the corner of the track it was time for me to take it up a notch. I began to build momentum and picked up my speed. As I picked up my speed, again as Coach predicted, the young ladies began to decrease in speed. The faster I ran the slower they became. The laughs that were once heard in the crowd turned into cheers. I did not allow the change in response to distract me but continue to run my race. As I ran, the young ladies that were once in front of me one by one moved behind me and I finished the race in first place.

Beautiful and Godly Lady, the bible teaches us in Matthew 20:16

So the last shall be first, and the first last: for many be called, but few chosen. God has assigned each and every one us our own race to run. It is our job to know what that race is and run it with all of our might. We must surround ourselves with Coaches that will give us godly wisdom to run our own race so that we don't fall for the trap of the enemy that tries to get us caught up in who is achieving more than us, or who is laughing at us. We must follow God's instructions for our lives and know that we are destined to win. God promises us that He will always cause us to triumph; now it our job to get in the race. We can win this thing. I believe in you.

Onward!

How will you release QUITTING?

BE FREE. BE YOU.

TRUST

> *Trust in the Lord with all thine heart and lean not unto thine own understanding. In all thy ways acknowledge him, and he shall direct thy paths.*
>
> — *PROVERBS 3:5-6*

Dear Beautiful and Godly Lady,

*Y*ou have to trust somebody! Easier said than done, huh? I know it all too well. These are the words my Bishop has said to me so many times. It is amazing the imaginary walls that we have constructed to keep people from our core. Like I said earlier, I get it. You were hurt. You were betrayed. You were lied on. You were cheated on. You were manipulated. Have I made it to your street yet? Again, I get it. There aren't a lot of women in this world that can say they have not experienced those things and more. However, those imaginary walls that we have developed are designed by the devil to keep us from experiencing the beauty of God's love from one person to the other. See, the walls not only keep us from giving love but they also hinder and prohibit us from receiving love.

And I am not just talking about the eros love or the erotic love from a man to a women, I am talking about the philos love from a friend to a friend or, most importantly, the agape love - the God kind of love. Imagine going through life not ever knowing what it means to give solely and completely of yourself, and always keeping people and God at arm's length. Imagine constantly looking over your shoulder for the imaginary dagger you think someone is trying to stab you in the back with. You keep thinking the illusive thought of *every person you meet is trying to get something from you* when the truth of the matter is they are really trying to get something to you. To think about it Beautiful and Godly Lady, are we really that vain? Are we really that narcissistic to put such value on ourselves to think that in this world of a billion people we are the only one that someone is out to get, to hurt, or to harm? Back to my original statement... *you have to trust somebody!* We have to be willing to trust God and be discerning enough to allow people into our lives. We have to open our hearts to experience new friendships, new relationships, and renewed and reestablished partnerships with people that can add to our lives, protect our lives, and correct our lives. We have to be willing to throw caution to the wind and say it is okay for me to trust you because I know you won't hurt me and I won't hurt you. Our paths are destined to support one another and build one another; and if by chance you do hurt me, it is not purposeful, you are human and I forgive you. Proverbs 3:5 teaches us to *Trust in the Lord with all thine heart and lean not unto thine own understanding. In all they ways acknowledge him, and he shall direct thy paths.*

Beautiful and Godly Lady, today I challenge you to knock the walls surrounding your heart down. Open the curtains of your soul so that God's light can shine in. Trust God to lead us to the right people at the right place and at the right time. Life is so much better when we are not alone. Let's learn to trust others, ourselves, and most of all God.

Onward!

BE FREE. BE YOU.

How will you release TRUST?

BE FREE. BE YOU.

WEIGHT

 For the battle is not yours, but God's.

— 2 CHRONICLES 20:15

Dear Beautiful and Godly Lady,

*I*f you know me, I carry huge bags because I am an electronics junkie so I need something to hold all my gadgets, plus my notebooks, and other essentials; as I deem them. Often times, I just throw things in my bag and rarely go back to clean out my bag. It wasn't like I did not know my bag was stuffed, because every time I picked it up to put it on my back, I could feel the weight getting heavier and heavier. Sometimes I would have to walk a little bent over because the weight of bag was so overbearing it was hurting my back. So one particular day I was attempting to put something in my bag; but my bag was so full I could not add anything else inside of it. Determined to get the item inside of my bag, I kept trying to force it in. However, the more I tried to push the paper inside the more it would cause the paper to crumble or tear which made me become frustrated, agitated, and aggravated. Being at the end of my rope, I finally said, "let me clean out my bag." So I braced myself, because I really was oblivious to the things inside my bag that could: one, cause it to be so heavy and two, not allow me to add anything else inside of it. As I took the time to remove items out of my bag and examine them, to my surprise, several pieces inside of my bag were not mine; as a matter of fact, those pieces were half the bag. I was housing papers and items that did not belong to me inside of my bag. I was hurting my back, carrying the weight of someone else's belongs. Now, that was the first half of the bag. When I continued to clean out my bagI discovered the other articles in my bag were outdated and I didn't need them anymore. Digging further, I noticed other pieces were just plain trash taking up space. By the time I finished, my bag was so light it was almost empty.

What am I saying? Beautiful and Godly Lady, often times in life we carry other people's weight. We are toting around their issues, their messes, their mishaps, and their anger as if it were our own. If we are not careful, we will allow those spirits to infect our spirit and we start to have an attitude towards others, and we don't know why. Our once happy go lucky demeanor is now unrecognizable. People are saying we have changed, and we insistently deny it; but the truth of the matter is we have changed. Association brings on assimilation and we have assimilated with spirits that were not good for who God called us to be.

Beautiful and Godly Lady, we are fighting battles that are not our battles to fight and we are starting wars that are not our wars to start. 2 Chronicles 20:15 reminds us *for the battle is not yours, but God's*. Because of the love and concern we have for our friends and loved ones, we sometimes posture ourselves as God and interfere with the lesson and the message God is teaching to that person. We are taking on what's not our problem. Release the weight. Give people back their stuff. There is a television show called *Hoarders* and the common statement of every person that is considered a hoarder is "it started out with one piece of something and then over time it multiplied and now it is out of control." Don't hoard other people's weight. We have enough on our own plates to manage. It's okay to give it back to them and allow God to do what he intended to do in the beginning. I promise you once you release the excess weight you will feel better. You will move better. You will sleep better and most of all, life will be better. I challenge you to try it and see. I know you can do it. I believe in you.

Onward!

What WEIGHT is holding you down? How will you release that weight?

BE FREE. BE YOU.

THANK YOU

> Giving thanks always for all things unto God and the Father in the name of our Lord Jesus Christ.
>
> — *EPHESIANS 5:20*

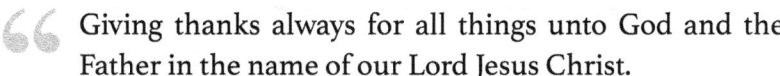ear Beautiful and Godly Lady,

I know you are probably saying how did "Thank You" become the last letter of the book? Surely "t" comes before "w" in the alphabet. Well, you are correct "t" does come before "w;" however, thank you should always be the last thing you say when you are graced with a gift from someone. My Bishop taught us that thank you always makes room for more. Yes, there will be an acknowledgement section in the book to thank everyone that supported me through this process; but I wanted to remind you Beautiful and Godly Lady that saying thank you will open more doors of favor than any other words can. Thank you expresses an appreciation for what has been done for us. Every day God grants us the opportunity for grace and for mercy and for that alone we should say thank you. Moving beyond the fact that God keeps us covered, he shields us from the consumption of the enemy and that is another reason we should say thank you. If that is not enough God prepares each day with a sufficiency to sustain us and holds us so that we can make it to the next day. For that alone we should say thank you. The list can go on and on. How about God not giving us what we deserved or God making a way out of no way.

Beautiful and Godly Lady, things may not always be the way we want them to be or occur in the timing that we want them to occur; but know that God's timing is always the right timing. Sometimes we get caught up in what we don't have and we miss the blessings of what we do have. There are so many women that wish they can switch places with you and have your life, have your shape, have your relationship, have your home, have your job, have your friends, have your love, and have your joy. God has us right where He needs us to be. So, if you haven't said it today, or if you haven't said it in a while, I challenge to stop reading for a second and look to the sky and tell the Lord thank you. Remember, thank you always makes room for more.

Onward!

What are you THANKFUL for?

BE FREE. BE YOU.

PRAYER

Father, I thank you for the women who read this book. I pray that something on inside of this book resonated with them. I pray that the anointing of the Holy Spirit empowered them through a story told or scripture used to ignite a fire to operate in their gifts, talents, and purpose. Thank you for using the women that have read this book to win souls for your kingdom. Thank you, Lord, for allowing women that have read this book to not be afraid to share their stories so that another woman may be set free. Thank you, Lord, for motivating any woman that have read this book to be free to be themselves and not be bound by judgement, ridicule, or the haunting of their past. I thank you Lord for any woman that have read this book and did not know you as their personal Lord and Savior but decided to accept you by confessing with their mouths and believing in their hearts that you died and were resurrected on the third day. Father, thank you for accepting anyone that walked away from you and is now returning back to their rightful place, which is in you. I thank you Lord for just being you. It is in Jesus name that I seal this prayer. Amen and it is so.

Onward!

Dr. Rox

NOTES

BE FREE. BE YOU.

BE FREE. BE YOU.

BE FREE. BE YOU.

BE FREE. BE YOU.

BE FREE. BE YOU.

www.ingramcontent.com/pod-product-compliance
Lightning Source LLC
Chambersburg PA
CBHW070554170426
43201CB00012B/1842